Hannah's Call to Care

How One Girl Discovered the Power of Protecting Wildlife

Claudia Clark

Author: Claudia Clark
Email: info@claudiaclarkauthor.com
Address:
Website: https://www.claudiaclarkauthor.com
SocialMedia:
https://www.facebook.com/profile.php?id=100063766662422
claudiaclarkauthor73 (Instagram)
https://www.linkedin.com/in/claudia-clark-7682492/
Claudia Clark - author, public speaker, wildlife warrior

Please direct all enquiries regarding books and school visits, virtual and real time, to the author.

Table of Contents

To Steve Irwin, Dr Jane Goodall, Sir David Attenborough, Greta Thunberg, Dian Fossey, and the other thousands of everyday citizens who tirelessly and bravely fought for the rights and protection of wildlife animals and their environment worldwide

Steve Irwin — 'We don't own the planet Earth; we belong to it. And we must share it with our wildlife.'

Jane Goodall— "What you do makes a difference and you have to decide what kind of difference you want to make."

Greta Thunberg— "You are never too small to make a difference."

About the Author

Claudia Clark is an author, speaker, activist, and animal lover focused on progressive causes. She has been obsessed with Australian wildlife since she saw her first photo of a koala as a young girl. After visiting Australia for the first time in 2023 and seeing kangaroos hop for the first time, she knew she needed to work to help protect these amazing animals.

In 2017, Claudia and her husband Brian moved from California to Germany, where she wrote her first book, *Dear Barack: The Extraordinary Partnership of Barack Obama and Angela Merkel.*

Claudia has advanced degrees focusing on public policy, social work, women's history, and labor relations. She is fluent in French and Spanish, has basic German knowledge, and enjoys reading, traveling, cooking, and spending time with her husband Brian and their ten-year-old labrador/shepherd rescue dog, Bella.

Acknowledgements

My deepest gratitude goes to my husband, Brian, for his love, support, and reinforcement throughout this project. Without his support, this book would never have been possible. I am also thankful for the love and respect for animals that my grandfather and mother instilled in me during my childhood, which inspired this book.

I would also like to thank my assistant, Mitzi Valentin, and my friends and supporters in Australia for their dedication to preserving Australia's endangered wildlife and their trust, support, and guidance as I undertook such a project. It would be difficult to acknowledge everyone who offered insight, but the following people provided incredible support and encouragement. Cybil Kaufmann, Pam Turner, Kylee Donkers, James Leonard, Stephen Dooley, Frances Carlton, Trish Rothville, Peter and Andrea Hylands, Maggie van Santen, Rob Daniel, Danielle Clode, Chris West, Shane Williams, Libby and Bec Fisher, and Kat and Malani from Koala Family Adventures.

A Wildlife Warrior

G'day **Mates!** My name is Hannah Stewart, and I am twelve. My parents call me their "Wildlife Warrior." I want to be a veterinarian when I grow up. Our class teacher tells me I am already a vet, and all I have to do to become qualified is continue listening, watching, and learning about what I love doing most.

I live with my attorney mum and architect dad in Leura, a small Australian town in New South Wales, tucked into the wild and beautiful Blue Mountains, about one hundred kilometres west of Sydney.

And yes, the mountains really are blue!

I am happy to live in Australia because our teachers tell us we have more unusual animals here than anywhere else in the world. From what I've seen, I believe it!

Everybody has heard of our most famous residents, the kangaroos, koalas, Tasmanian devils, and the unusual-looking platypuses. However, other fascinating creatures make their home here, and some have been here for millions of years, long before people arrived. When I watch them, I sometimes feel like a visitor to their world.

Animals with quirky names like pademelons, quokkas, ringtail possums, greater bilbies, sugar gliders, echidnas, wombats, dingoes, and flying foxes inhabit Australia. Many bird species, such as emus, swift parrots, pink and grey galahs, the irresistible kookaburras, and black cockatoos, loudly call Australia home.

Most people have to visit a zoo to see these animals, but we are lucky in Australia to have them living in our backyards, school playgrounds, and nearby bushland, close to where we work and play. They are generous and allow us to live in their world.

I have loved animals since I saw a koala clamber onto her mum's back while she climbed a tree. I was four and disappointed I could never have a cat or dog because my dad had severe allergies to them.

Then, on a summer day in March when I was eight years old, I had an experience that changed my life. I chose to become a vet so I would know how to help sick animals.

I was playing outside in the yard when Dad came home carrying a tiny kangaroo joey wrapped in a blanket. Excitedly, I peered at the furry bundle in his arms, and he told us he found her in her mum's pouch after she had been killed by a car. Mum heard us talking inside the house and came outside to see the excitement.

"Look at the baby kangaroo Dad brought me, Mum," I squealed.

"Yes, I see," she replied slowly, her eyes filled with concern or alarm.

"Can we keep her?" I asked innocently, looking anxiously between Mum and Dad, using my best 'get my own way' voice and look. "Kangaroos are not pets; they need to live in the wild," Dad told me gently but firmly.

"But she's too little and won't survive by herself. Let's keep her," I pleaded.

My father looked helplessly at Mum, who used the tactic all parents resort to when they need to say 'no' but don't know how.

"We'll see. In the meantime…," Mum added smoothly, changing the subject, "she must be hungry. Why don't we go inside and give her some warm milk."

Although Mum still sounded uncertain about the arrangement, she was practical and organised. "She'll need a name if we are going to keep her," she said, holding the door open.

"Because we found her in summertime, I think 'Summer' is the perfect name," Mum continued as we followed her inside.

I found a baby bottle I used for my dolls when I was younger and filled it with milk from our fridge. With Mum helping me to support the baby in my arms, I tried to feed Summer, but she wouldn't take the bottle.

"Maybe she prefers it warm," Mum reminded me, placing the bottle in the microwave for a few seconds before we tried again. It took nearly an hour, but Summer eventually drank most of the milk from the bottle we offered her and drifted off to sleep in my arms.

Dad found a pile of old towels, stacked them in a corner, and made a bed for her. Summer cried for her mother when she woke up. I desperately wanted to play with her, but Dad gently reminded me she needed rest. When I picked her up after dinner for another bottle, the towels were brown and wet from diarrhea.

"Eweee, that is disgusting," I exclaimed, unfortunately holding my nose with freshly wet fingers. Dad came over to see the cause of my small meltdown and laughed when he saw the mess I'd got myself into. "Taking care of animals needs plenty of work, and it's not always fun," he said kindly. He went into the kitchen, returning with paper towels and Wet Wipes, and handed them to me, saying it was my responsibility to clean her rear end and anywhere else that was messy.

We cared for Summer for the next three days, but my initial excitement about having a pet kangaroo soon faded. Summer was distressed from the moment we brought her home. She cried when she wasn't sleeping, and her tiny body trembled anytime I tried to play with her. Despite our efforts to feed her milk, she hardly drank it. Each time she took a few sips, it upset her tummy, and she had diarrhea again. Having a pet kangaroo wasn't as much fun as I thought it would be.

After lunch on the third day, Dad contacted a local wildlife rescue organisation he found online. He told them we were caring for a kangaroo joey and were concerned she wasn't doing well. He asked for their advice. The woman who answered the phone was friendly and promised a volunteer from their organisation would come to our house to examine Summer.

An hour later, Michelle from the local wildlife rescue arrived at our front door to check on Summer. Mum took Michelle into our living room, where Summer sat looking frightened and lonely. She explained how Dad found Summer in her mum's pouch after she had been struck by a car three days earlier and had brought her home to care for her. We tried to feed her cow's milk, but she didn't like it and became sick so we called for help.

Michelle examined Summer carefully. She looked at her ears and eyes, gently touched them, and tried to smooth her fur. I stood nervously behind Dad, peering out from behind him as Michelle assessed the sick Joey. Although she didn't say much during the examination, I could tell she was worried from her deep breaths and heavy sighs.

Finally, Michelle turned to us and explained, "I'm sorry to tell you that Summer is sick, and I need to take her with me so I can give her the medical care she needs." I began to sob, and Mum sat down on the couch to comfort me.

Michelle used a compassionate and professional voice to explain that kangaroos are wild animals and require special care, different from cats and dogs. Only people with specialised training are qualified to assist these animals.

"I know you were trying to help Summer, and that is wonderful, but unfortunately, some of that help did more harm than good.

"For example, kangaroos require a special formula because they are allergic to cow's milk. This is why Summer's stomach is upset; it couldn't digest the milk properly." Michelle explained that we were lucky because sometimes cow's milk can be so harmful to kangaroos it can kill them.

We learned the milk we fed to Summer wasn't our only mistake. Kangaroo joeys need the warmth and safety of their mother's pouch. Instead of leaving blankets on the floor, we should have used them to create a pretend pouch and hung them by the fireplace.

Michelle taught us that kangaroo joeys are naturally anxious animals and quickly become frightened as part of their defence mechanism in the bush. I didn't know this, but kangaroos are afraid of human sounds they don't hear in the wild, so things like the radio, TV, microwave, music, and even our voices can frighten them.

She mentioned that Summer's separation from her mum also created a lot of stress for her. "If you were taken somewhere unfamiliar, away from your family, given food that made you sick, and heard unfamiliar sounds, wouldn't you feel frightened?" Michelle asked, glancing at the blaring television.

I bit my lip and nodded, ashamed of my behaviour but Michelle reassured me,. "You haven't done anything others haven't. People think they are doing the right thing and only want to help these animals, but they need specialised care. When someone finds an animal in need, the first thing to do is contact a trained wildlife rescuer like me, preferably within twenty-four hours. This allows trained professionals to provide the necessary care, increasing the animal's survival chances. This is a legal requirement in Australia now, but most people don't know that."

As Michelle stood with Summer in her arms, through my tears, I explained, "I am so sorry. I only wanted to help; I didn't know I was hurting her."

Michelle smiled and hugged me. "I know that, and you are extremely kind. Here's the new plan," she said, becoming businesslike. "Summer will stay with me to recover until she is strong enough to survive in the wild on her own. I only live thirty minutes from here, so you can visit her anytime. Would you like that?"

"Oh yes, I would like that very much," I said, turning to my parents, who both nodded in support.

Since that afternoon, my parents have taken me to visit Michelle and her animal sanctuary every Saturday. Michelle and her husband, Greg, run a 7,500-acre sanctuary caring for injured and orphaned animals, including possums, koalas, wombats, flying foxes, lizards, birds, turtles, and sometimes snakes.

When I visit Michelle and Greg's sanctuary, I help with all the different jobs related to wildlife care, even the messy ones. I try to do a bit of everything except when it comes to snakes. I am still scared of them. Michelle tells me that snakes can be dangerous, but they are more afraid of humans than we are of them. I'm still not sure about that.

Michelle promises to teach me how to be safe around snakes when I'm ready. She emphasises that even though they may look scary, they play an essential part in the environment by eating insects, mice, and other animals that can harm plants and other wildlife. "When humans aren't around, there is a perfect balance in nature," she added, seeing I still looked doubtful.

Sometimes, I help Michelle sterilise bottles to feed the joeys. When I'm lucky, I get to bottle-feed them myself. Other times, I help Michelle or Greg by giving medication to sick animals or chopping fruit for the flying foxes. We also go "leaf browsing," searching the bush for special gum leaves to feed the koalas, who are extremely fussy about what they eat. We go on rescue missions when someone from the public calls and reports that they have found an injured animal that needs help. When that happens, we climb into their truck and drive to where the animal is. When we find the injured animal, we decide if it can be saved or needs euthanasia.

I used to cry every time we had to euthanise an animal, but Michelle told me that euthanasia was often the kindest and most humane thing to do. It was putting the animal out of its enduring pain and suffering.

It is sad, but I understand why we must do it. If the injured animal can be saved with love and medical care, we carefully secure it and take it back to the sanctuary. One time, when we rescued an abandoned baby possum, it had died by the time we got home and could get it settled. Sadly, that happens often, but when I get discouraged, Michelle reminds me about all the other animals we can and do save.

Each visit is different and enjoyable because I rarely do the same thing twice. However, one constant task is helping to clean up after the animals. One of the first things Michelle taught me was how to properly toilet the kangaroo joeys and how their mothers do it when the joeys are living in their pouches. This is important to prevent urinary tract infections. Since Joey's muscles aren't strong enough, mums stimulate their joeys to urinate and defecate by licking them after each feeding. In the absence of their mothers, humans must perform this task after each feed.

To stimulate the joey, gently but firmly rub the genital area with a tissue or toilet paper until the joey stops defecating and urinating. Wild animals produce a significant amount of waste that needs to be managed. Many animals also have enclosures that must be cleaned and raked several times daily.

While Michelle and Greg often ask me to help with the messy jobs, they encourage me to take part in fun activities, like feeding and playing with the animals. Whenever they have a wombat Joey in care, I take it outside, run around in circles, and watch it do zoomies. This is a lot of fun for me and is an important task to help the wombat get the exercise it needs to grow. And naturally, they love it too!

One day after I had volunteered with Michelle and Greg's for six months, and Michelle told me, "Today is the big day." I needed to help her clean the pen they'd built in their backyard because we were moving Summer and the other fourteen kangaroo joeys they had raised as the next step in preparing them for life in the wild.

Michelle explained that while the joeys still needed bottles for the next few months, she or Greg would frequently bring bottles to a feeding station. Here, the joeys could drink whenever they wanted to. This method was an essential step in reducing their contact with humans. By being outside, the joeys would learn to eat dirt, grass, and other natural foods, which helped them eventually become independent from the bottles. When that happened, we'd know they were weaned and could get all the nourishment they needed from being outdoors. After that, we'll open the gate, and the kangaroos will be free to come and go as they please.

"Many kangaroos are shy and will stay close for a while," Michelle told me. "Others hop away, and we never see them again. We never know what happens to them with those, but we hope for the best." Michelle handed me a rake to clean the dust and leaves from the ground.

"That is so sad," I said as I began to rake the area. "And joyful. *Bittersweet* is how I describe it," Michelle told me. "Kangaroos are wild animals and belong outdoors in the bush, not in our homes or backyards. The goal of caregivers is to raise and care for them so they can live as independent kangaroos in the wild. You'd be surprised how many return occasionally to hop in, say hello, grab a snack, and hop out again. One of the most rewarding aspects of rescuing animals is when mothers return with their Joeys, they want to show you."

Still sensing my sadness, she added, "Don't worry, we have a few more months before Summer is ready for that step." I returned to Michelle and Greg's ranch for the next five months, and life continued as usual. Then, one day, Michelle opened her door to let me in. "Today's the day," she told me. Even though the comment was vague, I knew what she meant. Today would be when we'd open the gate and give Summer and other joeys a chance to experience life in the wild.

Michelle hugged me as my eyes began to water. "You knew this day would come. This is a joyous occasion and means we've done our job well. Summer and the others are wild animals and belong in the bush with other kangaroos, not with humans. Thanks to our efforts, Summer can live a happy, free life in the wild, like all kangaroos should."

Michelle and Greg guided me through their house into the backyard and the pen where Summer and other mob members were resting. Greg looked over at the gate and then at me, indicating I should be the one to open it.

"I can't do it," I cried.

"Yes, you can. It is important for both you and Summer that you do this," Greg told me, placing his arm around my shoulder and gently guiding me until I was in front of the latch. My hands trembled as I opened the gate, and Greg nudged me out of the way as we watched the Joeys respond to this unexpected event.

We watched for several minutes. A couple of joeys hopped off quickly, and others stayed where they were but looked on curiously. Much to my sadness, Summer followed them after watching the more adventurous joeys hop away. Greg, Michelle, and I watched from the gate for a few minutes, and then Michelle turned and said, "Great job, well done! We have other animals we must attend to now." And that was that.

Whenever I came to Michelle and Greg's for the next two years, I asked if they had seen Summer. They shook their heads, and tired of the disappointment, I finally stopped asking. Then, one day, Michelle told me she had something to show me, a video she had captured on her phone. Summer had come to see her the day before with a surprise package. A joey in her pouch. Unfortunately, Summer hopped back into the bush before I arrived, but thanks to Michelle's quick thinking, I saw Summer again. She was happy and not only thriving in the wild but a new mother as well.

I enjoy spending time with Michelle, Greg, and the animals. I've learned that caring for wildlife requires a lot of quality time. Sometimes, I can't play with friends or visit my grandparents because I'm busy caring for the animals. I understand that not everyone shares my love for them or has the time to commit to their care as Michelle and Greg.

Sadly, because of many reasons like climate change, loss of habitat, conflict and competition between wild and domestic animals, and humans' misunderstanding of wildlife, many of Australia's most loved animals are at risk of extinction.

We are fortunate to live in a place with an abundance of beautiful and unique animals, and it is our responsibility to protect them. From my volunteer work with Greg and Michelle, I learned that caring for animals requires commitment and dedication. I understand that not everyone can be as involved in wildlife conservation as I am, but there are simple and effective ways we, as children and adults, can help protect all our precious animals.

Adults often remind us that we are the future. What better way to ensure a bright future than by protecting our wildlife?

Over the years, I have learned a lot from my experiences with Greg and Michelle. I want to share some of my experiences dealing with our wildlife's biggest and most urgent problems and the easy things we can do today to help everyone protect our animals.

What are Pouch Checks?

One of the first lessons I learned from Michelle is how to do a pouch check. I had only been volunteering with her for a few weeks when our phone rang after dinner one Saturday evening in April. Michelle received a call about an animal on the side of the road that had been hit, and someone asked her to check on it. Since the incident was close to our house, she thought this would be a good learning experience for me to go with her.

"Can I go?" I asked my parents eagerly.

"As long as you clean your room while you wait for Michelle," my mother told me firmly.

"But Mum," I began, "there isn't enough time."

Michelle told me that "time was of the essence," which sounded urgent, and I had to be ready when she arrived, or I wouldn't be allowed to go. "I promise I'll do it tomorrow."

"Nonsense, you have half an hour before she arrives. That is the deal."

"Okkkay," I groaned, but I quickly changed my tone as I gleefully told Michelle I would be waiting for her.

In record time, I made the bed, gathered a pile of clothes sitting on top of it for a week, tossed them into my dresser, and emptied my overflowing rubbish bin.

I was outside waiting for Michelle when she appeared. "What's first? What are we going to do?" I asked breathlessly.

Raising her eyebrows, she reversed out of the driveway. "I'm not sure. All the caller told me was that she saw a "rodent" on the roadside and asked someone to take care of it." She was cross at the caller's tone but grateful they'd made the effort. "I want to warn you," Michelle began, "the person who called about the animal was not the one who hit it, so if we find it, it's likely to be in bad shape. We may not be able to save it."

I was grateful for the warning. "Why don't people call when they hit an animal?" I asked innocently.

"Lots of reasons," Michelle said. "Sometimes it's laziness, others are unaware they hit the animal, and sadly, others are afraid to call", Michelle continued.

"What are people afraid of?" I asked.

"Consequences: because many of Australia's native animals are endangered and therefore protected, people are scared they will get into trouble with the police for hitting one."

"They won't?" I asked, fascinated with this new information.

"No, of course not. Accidents happen. We cannot fault people for that, but we can blame them for being irresponsible and not calling for help. Most of the time, when we receive calls about an animal injured by a car, it is from someone other than the driver, like in this case. Time is crucial, and any delay in getting the animal treatment can mean the difference between life and death."

Michelle sighed as she continued, "People also see a koala climb a tree and a kangaroo or wallaby hopping off after being struck. They assume the animal is okay, but these are the animal's instincts, and they will do them regardless of how injured they are. That is why all animals hit by vehicles must be reported so we can go and examine them."

"But what if you're not able to find them?" I asked.

"That happens a lot, but rescuers go out and spend time searching. Sometimes, we find them, and sometimes, we don't. Exactly what we are doing now," Michelle smiled kindly. "Let's hope we find this one." Michelle said optimistically

We drove about five kilometres to the road sign landmark, where the caller told Michelle the "rodent" could be found. Michelle parked the car by the side of the road, turned on her headlights and hazard lights, and told me to be careful. And while I was getting out of the car, she slipped on her hi-vis vest.

"Stay here for a second," she cautioned me, opening the boot and handing me a high-vis vest, too. The vest was so big on me that I looked ridiculous. Hiding a smirk, Michelle sensed my embarrassment and said, "Nobody will recognise you. We can get one that fits you better later. Besides you are here to help an injured animal not participate in a fashion show" she kidded.

Luckily, the caller gave Michelle good instructions about the animal's location, and we spotted the wombat easily. Breathing deeply, Michelle told me the wombat hadn't survived the accident. However, because wombats are marsupials, we needed to check whether the animal were a male or female.

If this were a female, we would check her pouch to see if she had a live joey inside. As we examined the animal, Michelle reminded me that only female marsupials have pouches. As we examined it, Michelle showed me that because there were no testicles, the deceased animal was a female, and we needed to check her pouch.

I watched as she opened the pouch and pinched the fur between her hands and lifted her so she could stretch the opening to get a better look inside. Neither of us initially saw anything, but Michelle said newborns can be extremely tiny and difficult to spot. She took the torch I had been holding, and we both looked closely.

Neither one of us could see a joey. "Are we finished?" I asked.

"No, we need to check the teats, and if one is longer than the other, it's possible the mother was feeding her baby when she was struck."

Finding nothing unusual, Michelle put her finger close to her lips to indicate I needed to be quiet, and she motioned for me to remain still. We stayed silent, not moving for ten minutes. When Michelle determined it was safe, she explained, "We wait and listen to hear a joey calling for their mum. When they do, it sounds like a squeaky or grunting noise, but it's a quiet sound, so we must stay still to hear it and not frighten the joey further."

After ten minutes and no noise or sign of a joey, Michelle declared it we could safely move the wombat further into the bush to prevent scavenging wildlife from being run over by passing vehicles. Michelle carefully placed some tree branches over the wombat, and we waited a couple of minutes out of respect for the animal before we began to return to the car.

When we walked back to the car, I asked Michelle why the caller had referred to the wombat as a "rodent". Inhaling deeply and choosing her words carefully, she responded, "Well, agriculture is a big industry in Australia, and because wombats, by nature, love to dig and burrow, they destroy the rabbit-proof fences farmers install to keep rabbits from destroying the crops and soil. It is unfortunate because wombats, like all animals, play an essential role in our ecosystem."

"How is moving dirt from one place to another beneficial?" I asked naively.

Michelle laughed, "That's a good question, and one adults don't even understand. When wombats dig or burrow, it may look as if they are simply moving dirt around, but what that does is it brings necessary nutrients to the surface, which helps cultivate hard soils and new vegetation to grow."

"So it's like they are recycling the dirt?" I asked.

"In a sense, yes." Michelle told me. "Now you have a good response next time you hear anyone refer to wombats as pests, nuisances or rodents."

Even though Michelle and I didn't find a joey during this trip, it was an excellent experience because I learned how to do a pouch check. Sadly, it was not long before we went out on a call and had to rescue a kangaroo joey—just like my father had done with Summer. This is a common occurrence. I thought about keeping a journal of all the rescues we attended and the number of joeys we found, but in the middle of a rescue, things were so crazy that it was too much for me to think about.

Australia is home to 330 marsupial species, nearly two-thirds of all marsupial species worldwide. How cool is that? As we learn in school, marsupials are unique animals in which the mother has a pouch where her baby, called a joey, develops until it can live independently. Examples of marsupials include kangaroos, koalas, wombats, possums, and even the Tasmanian devil.

When riding in the car with your parents, have you noticed a dead animal on the side of the road with a big "X" marked on it with spray paint or a marker pen? Did you wonder what it means? This marking tells other drivers that someone has already checked the animal's pouch for a joey, so no one else needs to.

People should do this because joeys can survive inside their mother's pouch for several days if something happens to her. That's why it's important to check a marsupial's pouch and the area around her if you come across a dead female marsupial, like a wombat, koala, or kangaroo, on the road or in the wild.

If you're unsure how to check a pouch, many wildlife rescue organisations have online videos providing step-by-step instructions. These videos demonstrate how to determine if a mother has a joey, remove it safely if one is present, and care for it until you can get it to a professional who will provide proper care.

If you are brave enough to check the pouch yourself (or are with adults who can do it) and find a joey, contacting the appropriate wildlife organisation immediately is essential. They can start the process of helping the animal as soon as possible.

If you find it too scary to check a pouch yourself, you can ask your parents or the adults with you for help. Alternatively, if you are alone, you can call a wildlife rescue organisation and inform them of your location and what you have found. The person on the phone may ask you to stay near the animal until help arrives.

If that is not possible, you can cover the animal with something to make it easier for rescuers to identify it. This small action could help the rescuers and save the animal's life.

When people arrive, they can check for a joey and assess whether it can be saved with proper care and attention. If they believe the joey can survive with help, they will take it to a veterinarian or someone like Michelle and Greg, who will provide care until it is big enough to be released back into the wild.

Pouch-checking is a crucial way to help protect our wildlife. It doesn't require any money, training, or long-term commitment. It is easy to do and can be performed by anyone, making it valuable for safeguarding our marsupials.

Domestic Pets Versus Wildlife

One of the saddest animals I helped Michelle and Greg care for was a koala a dog had attacked. I remember showing up one Saturday to volunteer and saw a koala in the area Michelle and Greg referred to as "the intensive care" unit. The sickest animals or those requiring the most care stayed in this area. Usually, when I arrive, I typically go around the property and take an inventory of the animals in care, note the progress they have made since I saw them last, and ask about new arrivals.

I saw a male koala with an ugly-looking bite on his eye and several equally savage cuts all over his body. "What on earth happened?" I asked, horrified, examining the latest addition to the wildlife hospital.

"Dog attack," Greg told me flatly. Seeing the confused look on my face, he added, "Tragically, it often happens. A dog off lead attacked the koala as he attempted to cross the road. Luckily, a member of the public witnessed everything and called us immediately. Michelle went and retrieved him and took him to the vet. Dog attacks often cause serious and even fatal internal injuries. The x-rays showed that 'Buster's' injuries are superficial, so with medication to prevent an infection and ointment to help the wounds heal, he'll be okay, and we'll get him back to his home."

Do you know the difference between domestic animals and wild animals? Domestic animals can live with humans and often require our assistance to survive. They rely on us for food, shelter, and care. Cats and dogs are perfect examples of domestic animals.

In contrast, wild animals live outdoors in environments like the bush, forests, coastlines, and deserts. These species do not depend on humans for survival and prefer to avoid contact with us. While many wild animals fear humans, some can pose a danger to people. Examples of wild animals include kangaroos, dingoes, reptiles and many species of birds.

Because domestic and wild animals have different lifestyles and diets, they sometimes compete, posing risks to both wildlife and domestic animals. Keeping these two groups separate is challenging because we all share the same planet. However, we can take steps to help protect one from the other.

It takes thousands of years for animals to develop defence mechanisms against new threats. Cats and dogs are not native to Australia. They were brought by explorers on the First Fleet in 1788. In scientific terms, dogs and native Australian animals have only had a short time to interact, and many native animals have not yet learned to be afraid of dogs. Unfortunately, dog attacks are one of the biggest threats koalas face. Each year, more than one hundred koalas are attacked and killed by dogs. Although this number is alarming, there are actions we can take to reduce it.

Dog attacks can happen on public and private property; preventing this can differ depending on where you live. A meaningful way to reduce the risk is to enrol your dog in obedience training, especially programs that teach them to avoid other animals and always return to you on command. This will help minimise contact and conflicts with koalas and other wildlife.

I understand how much we want our pets to be free to explore their environment, but keeping your dog on a lead is essential, especially when walking where koalas live. Keeping your dog on a lead, you're helping protect your best friend and the vulnerable wildlife. This way, you can feel relaxed knowing you have better control over your dog, ensuring they stay close and don't accidentally wander into koala habitats or chase after one. It's about creating a safe and enjoyable experience for everyone.

Most attacks on koalas happen in residential backyards. While dog attacks can happen at any time of year, they are most frequent between August and February. This increase in attacks is mainly due to the koalas being more active during their breeding season, searching for mates and coming down from their trees.

Since koalas are nocturnal and, therefore, more active at night, dog attacks happen more frequently during these hours. To help prevent attacks, a straightforward solution is to limit your dog's activities at night. Keep your dogs inside after dark, and if you need to take your pet outside, use a lead.

If you would rather not keep your dog indoors, there are other things, such as kennels and enclosures, to confine your dog. If confining your dog is not possible, another effective option is to use koala exclusion fencing to keep koalas out of your yard. There are many different types of fencing, and if you or your parents go to government websites, you will find information about fencing designed to keep koalas out.

Unfortunately, as careful as we are, accidents happen, and a dog attacks a koala. When that happens, there are steps you should take to improve the koala's chances of survival.

It's essential to remember that everyone, especially police officers and rescuers, understands that accidents do happen. If a dog attacks a koala on its property, dog owners should not be afraid to come forward. We know that feelings of fear, guilt, or shame can make it difficult to report such incidents. Still, it's essential to recognise that police officers and wildlife caregivers see the situation as simply a dog defending its territory, acting on its instinct.

Remember, animals often don't show visible signs of injury, so it's crucial to have them evaluated by a professional as soon as possible to make sure they are OK. That is why it is essential to call a local wildlife organisation when you remove the dog from the scene of an attack.

Because koalas are marsupials, you should check the pouch, and if there is a joey present, it can be treated and released back into the wild when it is healthy enough.

If the koala is alive, you should avoid interfering until a wildlife carer arrives. Still, you can temporarily confine it by placing an upturned box, washing basket, or large bin on top with a weight on top.

While koalas are adorable, it's important to note that they may bite or scratch with their sharp teeth and claws, especially when injured or frightened. You should protect yourself if you need to help a koala and get it to a wildlife carer or veterinarian. It's wise to wear thick, long gloves that cover your forearms to protect yourself while being gentle with the koala.

Wrapping the koala in a soft towel or blanket can help keep it calm and secure, making the process easier for both of you. When placing the koala in a sturdy cardboard box, add a hessian bag or towel at the bottom to give it something to grip onto. Handle the koala quickly but gently to minimise its stress and discomfort, always remembering that kindness and empathy are key when caring for these precious creatures.

One afternoon during the school holidays, Michelle invited me to visit her sister, who lives outside Sydney. She thought it would be nice for me to see Sydney, and she had a nephew my age with whom I could play. When we arrived, Michelle's twelve-year-old nephew, Scott, greeted us at the door. He excitedly took me to the backyard to show me his tree house.

However, to his disappointment, it was not his tree house that intrigued me, but rather the giant screened-in porch fixture that took up most of the backyard. Putting my face against the screen for a better view, I saw two of the largest cat jungle gyms I had ever seen. Heaps of cat toys were scattered with a fresh litter box, and two cats were curled up asleep on either side of the food and water bowls. I am not exaggerating when I say the enclosure was bigger than my and my parents' bedrooms combined. "What on earth?" I asked.

"It's a cat enclosure," Scott responded in a tone that indicated I had asked the dumbest question he'd ever heard.

"I see that, but why?" I asked, still bewildered, as I had never seen anything elaborate.

"My parents think it's inhumane to confine cats indoors, and because cats are dangerous to many native animals, this gives them a chance to be outside without killing the wildlife," Scott explained. "So Aunt Michelle suggested we have one installed."

I could tell from his tone that he was surprised I had never seen one. "They are becoming popular in the city. When we first got this, nobody else had one, but now all my friends with cats have them," he explained. "They come in all different sizes, and I'm proud ours is the biggest one I've seen," Scott continued. I was so impressed by this castle-like feature I almost wanted a cat so we could have one of these enclosures.

Cats hold a special place in our hearts and are cherished family members. I was always disappointed we could never have a cat because my dad was allergic to them. I know people love their cats, and I am not suggesting we get rid of them. However, people need to understand the threat they are to our wildlife.

Since Europeans introduced cats to Australia in 1788, the feral cat population has grown between 2.1 to 6.3 million. On top of those numbers, people have an additional 3.8 million cats as pets, many of which can wander freely outdoors. Scientists have noted that cats have sadly played a role in the extinction of 27 species, including unique native rodents, potoroos, bandicoots, bilbies, wallabies, and several bird species. It's a complicated situation that calls for both compassion for our pets and consideration for wildlife conservation.

One of the simplest and healthiest choices you can make for your cat is to keep it indoors. This prevents your cat from wandering outside, helping to protect it from encounters with wildlife and reducing the risk of accidents, such as being hit by a car. Additionally, keeping your cat indoors lowers the chances of it contracting diseases, like the parasite Toxoplasmosis, which needs early detection and treatment with antibiotics.

Desexing your cat, taking it to the vet for its vaccinations, and regular check-ups are other ways to help ensure your cat lives a long, healthy life. Additionally, desexing your cat is a compassionate choice that shows you care about their well-being and helps minimise any negative impact they or their offspring have on local wildlife.

Many believe pets deserve to roam freely outdoors and that keeping cats indoors is cruel or restrictive. If your parents or neighbours feel this way, some compromises allow cats greater access to roam without jeopardising the safety of wildlife.

One simple and affordable way to help protect wildlife while allowing your cat outdoor time is to place three large bells on their collar, two under the chin and one on the opposite side. While it's important to acknowledge that bells aren't the solution, they impact about one out of three predatory attempts, therefore offering a level of awareness for nearby animals and birds that danger lurks, which can make a difference.

If you have a cat-proof fence, you can create cat-free zones in your yard. Use a "floppy wire" fence to enclose shrubs and trees, providing safe spaces for wildlife. Adding nectar-producing plants and a water source can also attract birds. However, if you let your cat roam and have installed bird baths, place them where cats can't reach them to prevent birds from being lured into danger. If a safe spot isn't available, removing the birdbath is best.

Cat enclosures are the latest trend for animal lovers. They offer an exciting way to let our feline friends enjoy the great outdoors while ensuring wildlife stays safe. There are many options to choose from. You can find dedicated organisations specialising in making free-standing or attached enclosures. You can creatively transform existing spaces, like unused aviaries or garages, into fantastic cat adventure parks. Whichever option you choose, it is the perfect combination of adventure and safety for your pets and the wildlife.

Among the many options available, a proper enclosure can transform your cat's experience, whether for overnight or longer stays when you are on holiday. Creating a space that provides food, fresh water, a clean litter box, and a warm, dry sleeping area is essential for shorter stays. For more extended stays, an enclosure should include those basics and encourage exercise and exploration. This cat tower features multiple sleeping spots at different heights, a towering scratching and climbing pole that reaches up to 2.5 meters tall, and inviting perches for lounging. You can add fun cat toys to encourage daily play, running, and jumping. Additionally, consider adding window perches for sunbathing or a cat door that leads to a secure outdoor area.

I know this is a lot to think about, and many factors play a part in deciding whether or which cat enclosure would be right for your furry friend. A Land for Wildlife extension officer, local veterinarian, RSPCA, and Cat Protection Society can provide more advice on confining your cat or building an enclosure. It is important to know that many of these alternatives are safe, effective, and easily helpful ways to help our domestic cats live peacefully with our wild animals.

Barbed Wire Fences

Whenever the opportunity presents itself, I try to teach what I learned from Michelle and Greg to my friends, family, classmates, and teachers. For example, one day, my best friend Miranda and I were walking to school, and we saw a flying fox tangled in a fence outside a grocery store.

Upon hearing me screech in horror, "Oh no!" Miranda followed me. I fought my urge to retrieve the animal since I was not vaccinated against the Australian Bat Lyssavirus (ABLV). I knew that if I touched it, I would either have to lie to my parents and risk them forbidding me from ever helping Michelle again or tell my parents the truth and getting lectured by both my parents, Michelle and Greg.

Even though the chances of getting bitten by the flying fox are remote, Michelle has always been firm that, as a precaution and until I am vaccinated, I am not allowed to touch them. Luckily, I could still see the injured animal as I ran towards the fence for a better view. Miranda followed me.

I kept my distance but got close enough to assess the situation. "It's only a bat," Miranda told me, perturbed by my distress. "Who cares. They are smelly and bite people," she added dismissively.

"I care, and that is not true," I replied stubbornly. "They are cute and play an important role in our environment. We need to protect them," I said, as I looked for my phone in my backpack.

"What are you doing?" Miranda asked, annoyed. "We're going to be late for school."

"I am going to call wildlife rescue and ask them to come and rescue the bat, and I'll wait here until they arrive," I said.

"You cannot be serious. We'll get into so much trouble," Miranda pleaded as I called Wildlife Rescue to tell them about the bat and our location. "It wouldn't be the first time," I admitted. "Besides, my parents won't be mad at me if I am late for something like this," I said. "You go ahead if you're scared."

She rolled her eyes and sighed. "No, I'll stay," she said.

"Good, now you can help me find a towel or blanket to put over the bat to protect it until the rescuer arrives." I noticed the grocery store was open. "I'll go and ask them if they have anything while you stay here with the bat," I said, turning towards the store.

"No, you stay here, I'll go ask," Miranda said hurriedly.

Miranda returned a couple of minutes later with a tea towel, which I carefully placed over the injured animal. A few minutes later, a man from the local bat rescue centre arrived, gently untangled her from the fence, and thanked us for our help.

"Is she going to make it?" I asked.

"I'm not sure," he answered truthfully, "but she has a chance, thanks to your call." The volunteer promised to tell me about the flying fox's condition before he drove away.

I looked nervously at the time as Miranda and I walked to school. We were twenty minutes late, and Ms. Davis, our principal, was waiting for us when we opened the doors.

"School starts at 8:00, not 8:20," she told us sternly.

"I know, and we are sorry," I began, "but…"

"This is the third time this year. We will have to inform your parents about this," she said, directing us into her office. "I warned you."

"But Ms. Davis," I continued, "we were waiting for a volunteer from Animal Rescue to arrive because we found a flying fox caught in barbed wire," I replied, in a tone begging for understanding.

"And that's the third time you have used that excuse this year," Ms. Davis told me. "I need to call your parents. You knew the consequences of being late again," Ms. Davis said crossly.

"The next time I see an injured animal that needs care, what am I supposed to say? *I'm sorry I could help you, but I won't because I'll be late for school.*" I asked as we sat nervously on two chairs in her office.

"That is enough with the attitude, Miss Stewart," Ms. Davis said sternly.

"My mum is going to be so angry," Miranda whispered while we waited.

"Don't worry," I assured her, "my mum will fix this."

Luckily, my mum's law office is only ten minutes from our school, and she happened to be there and not in court when Ms. Davis called.

"Mrs. Stewart, Hannah's mum?" Ms. Davis began, then not waiting for a reply, "Punctuality is an essential part of a student's academic career, and tardiness is unacceptable, do you agree?"

"I understand that," my mum said calmly, "and if the girls had been late because they were dawdling or getting into trouble, then yes, I would agree. However, Hannah messaged to say they found an injured animal on the way to school and wanted to stay with it until help arrived. I believe that is admirable behaviour, don't you, Ms. Davis and the girls should be rewarded rather than punished for their actions?"

"Wellll…" Ms. Davis hesitated, seeing that she was already losing her case but didn't want to lose face too, "Don't let it happen again. School must come first." "Social studies can wait a few minutes; an injured animal cannot," my mum retorted, not backing down. "Remind me again of the school motto, please, Ms. Davis: *Learning with Kindness, Caring, Support,* isn't it?" Ms. Davis had been unable to contact Miranda's parents, so Mum added," I will speak to Miranda's parents this evening and advise her about what happened today," she added authoritatively.

Ms. Davis knew when she'd been beaten. "I think we have wasted enough time on this matter. You girls should get to class."

Later that night, when I was doing my homework, Miranda called to tell me my mum had called and explained what had happened, and everything was ok. Miranda asked if I had heard about the bat's condition from the organisation.

"Why do you care? After all, it was *just a bat*," I teased her gently.

"I'm sorry, you were right, it was kinda cute." Miranda sighed. "I hope it was ok."

"Yes, I called when we returned from school, and they had to euthanise it. Her wing was broken, and they couldn't repair it," I said.

"So, we did that all for nothing," Miranda said, sounding defeated.

"No, it wasn't for nothing. The bat would have stayed entangled for hours in terrible pain before someone else came along or before it died from its injuries. We saved the bat from hours of suffering. It's not the worst outcome," I said practically, "and I'll do the same again whenever I find an injured animal."

Barbed wire fences serve several important purposes, including keeping pets safe, protecting them from potential intruders, and providing privacy from strangers. Despite these benefits, barbed wire is a deadly trap for our wildlife. Recent veterinary reports show they have treated over eight hundred native Australian animals during the last year, including owls, gliders, kangaroos, koalas, and tawny frogmouths, from fence-related injuries.

Among these species, the flying fox is particularly affected, with more than half of the reported injuries, over four hundred, occurring in this species. Alarmingly, around 80% of these flying foxes did not survive their injuries.

You may have heard adults say negative things about flying foxes. Things like they smell, are dirty, or carry rabies, which is harmful to people. Flying foxes do carry a virus called Australian Bat Lyssavirus (ABLV). It is similar to rabies, but not the same. People can catch the virus from an infected bat, but the chances of that happening are extremely rare.

Since ABLV is transmitted from infected bats to humans through bites, scratches, or contact with saliva or neural tissue to broken skin or mucous membranes, such as the eyes, nose, and mouth, the safest way to avoid ABLV is not to touch bats. This is easy because they don't like being touched anyway. Luckily, humans can get vaccinated to protect them from getting sick if they work with flying foxes.

Despite their bad reputation, flying foxes are amazing animals that play a critical role in preserving our environment. They are nocturnal animals and leave their homes or roost at dusk to find food. They are known to fly up to fifty kilometres every night looking for food, always camp near rainforests, and disperse across twenty-six species of rainforest canopy trees.

They are key to the environment because, while flying, they distribute seeds in their droppings and carry pollen from tree to tree, fertilising flowers as they feed. Eucalypts rely heavily on these pollinators, producing most of their nectar and pollen at night to coincide with when bats are active. Without flying foxes, there is less cross-pollination between trees, particularly over long distances, and fewer seeds are spread. Fewer seeds equals fewer trees.

Flying foxes are primarily active after dark. Unfortunately, they often cannot see barbed-wire fences and struggle to avoid them, especially in windy conditions. When they collide with this lethal obstacle, they can hit it at speeds of 35 to 40 kilometres per hour. This leads to serious injuries as they twist and fight against the wire, desperately trying to chew their way out.

Once trapped, most bats struggle even more to escape, resulting in greater entanglement. Many of these bats sustain severe injuries, including broken bones, damage to their wing membranes, and horrific mouth injuries caused by their attempts to free themselves by chewing on the wire or their wings.

Barbed wire fences hurt wildlife, so it's best to avoid using them in areas where wildlife can get caught, especially on the top strand. Fortunately, many safer alternatives offer the same benefits as traditional fences without harming wildlife. For example, consider planting a row of native trees or shrubs or using a split polypipe over the barbed wire, particularly in areas where trees or bushes are growing through the fence.

For fencing, use single-strand white horse sighter wire or paling fences. You can also add some shade cloth over the top strand of barbed wire and mark it with white UV-stabilised poly tape. Wider tape is better because the white colour helps visibility at night.

It's best not to plant flowering or fruiting trees or shrubs near barbed wire, as these attract hungry flying foxes.

In addition to changing the type of fencing you use, being vigilant about wildlife and its surroundings is crucial. For example, check all fences every morning for trapped animals and contact a rescue group immediately if you find one. The longer a bat remains entangled in wire, its injuries become more serious. Call a bat rescue organisation immediately if you see a bat caught in barbed wire. If possible, without touching the bat, gently throw a towel over it to help calm it down during this stressful time. Your compassion can make a big difference in their recovery.

Wildlife is a precious part of our surroundings, and it's something we all should take a role to protect them.. With the abundance of animals surrounding us, it can feel overwhelming to consider protecting them all. No individual can do this task alone, but if we commit to being mindful and caring, we collectively increase our chances of noticing and aiding injured wildlife.

Together, our small efforts make a significant difference in the lives of these incredible creatures. Making a difference to one makes a world of difference for that animal.

Understanding the different types of fences and materials can be challenging. It is okay not to have all the answers about every kind of fence available. What matters is recognising how barbed wire poses a risk to all wildlife. Sharing this information with friends, family, and teachers will help raise awareness about safer alternatives that protect wildlife. Your efforts make a meaningful difference for the animals that share our world.

Let's Build a Possum Box

My enthusiasm for wildlife has led teachers, neighbours, and community members to frequently seek my advice on native animals. I enjoy this, as it makes me feel knowledgeable and valued. More importantly, it shows that people are listening to me and changing their attitudes and behaviours toward our precious wildlife.

While Miranda and I were riding our bikes in the neighbourhood one afternoon, my retired banker neighbour, Mr. Milton, stopped me. "Hannah, a mother opossum and a bunch of her babies are living in my garage. How do I get rid of them?" he asked, sounding hostile.

Biting my lip to maintain my composure, I calmly asked, "How do you know a possum is living in your garage?"

"It started a few weeks ago when we heard a lot of scratching, ripping, and scuttling sounds. We thought it was mice, so we investigated but didn't see anything. Then, the noise disappeared, and we didn't think much of it.

"However, a couple of weeks later, we began hearing hissing and shrieking noises, along with other strange sounds." Mr. Milton mimicked it by putting his lips together and smacking them. "Of course, we became suspicious and wanted to know where the noise came from.

"Lo and behold, last night, we came home and caught the mother eating our cat's food. We must have startled her because she looked up from the bowl, glanced at us, and then continued eating while her babies were still on her back." Mr Milton sounded irritated. "So now, tell me, how do I get rid of her?" he asked emphatically.

I glanced at Miranda, who covered her mouth to stifle her laughter before I replied. "First of all, Mr. Milton," I began, and I heard Miranda mutter under her breath, "Here we go," as she gave up her battle and burst into laughter. She knew the lecture I was about to give and waited for the words to come pouring out of my mouth.

"It is illegal to relocate possums more than fifty meters. They are territorial animals and do not adjust to being moved and often don't survive when this happens," I began.

He gave me a look that suggested he regarded them as pests, and no one cared if they lived or died. It was a look I had seen far too often, but I continued doggedly, "Contrary to popular opinion, possums are not pests; they play an essential role in our ecosystem. They are also natural rubbish disposals; bugs and insects are a primary part of their diet.

They form an essential link in the food chain because they are prey for larger predatory animals, are immune to bee and scorpion stings, and are resistant to the venom of most snakes. "Additionally, something most people don't know, they contribute to seed dispersal. As possums move around foraging for food, seeds from plants stick to their fur or are passed through their digestive system. This happy accidental transportation of seeds helps propagate many plant species, aiding in maintaining biodiversity in our ecosystems."

"They scare my cat and eat her food," Mr. Milton countered angrily.

"Maybe a simple solution would be to place your cat's food in the house," I suggested logically.

"That's enough of the attitude, Hannah. What do I do about this? I don't want possums living in my garage."

"The first thing you need to do," I suggested, staying patient and ignoring *his* attitude like I had seen Michelle and Greg do many times in similar situations, "is find where the possum is entering and exiting. When you know that, then seal off the area, but before you do that, build a comparable box for the possum to use as its new home," I stated matter of factly.

"I don't know how it's getting in," Mr. Milton said irritably, shrugging his shoulders.

"What if my friend and teacher, Michelle, came over to check out the garage with me? Maybe we can find a way of helping you and the possums live happily together."

"As long as it happens sooner rather than later," he nodded gruffly.

After Miranda and I finished our bike ride, I called Michelle and told her about my recent conversation. She had an emergency with one of the animals at home, so she sent Greg to investigate.

I met Greg at Mr. Milton's house, and Greg examined the garage area fully. There was a particularly dirty area in the garage next to a bush that rested against it.

"This is where the possum is coming in," Greg said firmly, "but to be certain, watch this area just after dark to see if the possum leaves. Once she leaves for the night, and as long as she has her babies, you need to use timber or solid sheeting to seal the hole," Greg explained.

"I don't have any of that but chicken wire. Can I use that?" Mr. Milton asked.

"Unfortunately, no, the possum can easily pull the wire away with its claws and get back in," Greg continued.

"How do I get the possum to stay out of the garage?" Mr. Milton asked.

"Keep a light on in there for several days and nights because they prefer to sleep in the dark; this might deter them." Mr. Milton nodded.

"When the possum is out, you must seal that entry point. Otherwise, you will have other possums moving in before you know it," Greg smiled.

"Once I get it out, then what do I do if I'm not allowed to relocate it?" Mr. Milton asked, sounding irritated again.

"I suggest you provide an alternative home by building a sturdy weatherproof possum box, and placing it high enough in the tree the possum will be out of reach for cats or dogs," Greg suggested.

39

"Oh yes, I remember Hannah mentioned something about that," he admitted. "How do I encourage it to move to its new home?" Mr. Milton asked. He began to sound more interested than irritated.

"Place fruit like pears, grapes, or apples near the box to tempt the possum into investigating its potential new home."

"Okay, thank you for your help," Mr. Milton said, shaking Greg's hand as they headed to the driveway.

"One more thing," Greg added, peering at the tree branches near the garage, "trim these to make it more difficult for possums to access the garage."

"Okay, I can do that. I am not sure about being able to seal off the entry point. Would you be willing to do that for me?" he asked.

"I'd be happy to," Greg said. "Call me when you're sure the possum has gone."

I feared that Mr. Milton would be too quick to seal the entry off before the possum found a new home, so I suggested, "I have an idea. Why don't I ask at school if we could get credit for building possum boxes? You and Michelle receive more and more requests for them, so why not have plenty on hand for situations like this?" I asked.

"Aren't there places where you can buy them already made?" Mr. Milton asked.

"Yes, there are," Greg responded, "but I like that idea of kids constructing their own. It gives them an opportunity to actively contribute to helping our wildlife. We have room at our place to store them," Greg agreed.

"Do you honestly think a bunch of kids are going to give up their spare time for something like that?" Mr. Milton asked skeptically.

"You'd be surprised…" I said, "Especially if they can receive credit for it."

Realising all his objections had been easily and charmingly knocked over, Mr. Milton begrudgingly agreed he would wait until we installed the new box before evicting the possum from his garage. "If you think you can do it ..."

"Oh, we'll do it. You can be sure of that," I smiled proudly.

On Monday, when I arrived at school and asked Mr. James, our science teacher, about the possibility, he shook his head regretfully, "I am sorry, we don't have the time or resources to do it here, but if you find somewhere else, I'll gladly give school credit to any students who participate," he agreed.

I was disappointed but not defeated. My dad was a good handyman, and this might be a project he would get behind. When I approached him with the idea, he didn't hesitate to agree to host the event and donate the necessary materials. Two weeks later, fifteen classmates, along with Greg, Michelle, and Mr. James to chaperone and assist, spent a Saturday afternoon constructing fifteen possum boxes.

After we completed the project, Greg and I went to Mr. Milton's house to install our handiwork. "I have to hand it to you, Hannah. This is very well done. I am impressed with your commitment. I never thought you'd see this through; it is refreshing to see young kids passionate about something," he said admiringly.

"You can always count on Hannah to follow through with her promises about helping wildlife," Greg said proudly. "Now, as promised, I will seal that hole for you, and with any luck, the possum will prefer its new home to your garage."

Possums are common across Australia, and some states may have different laws about relocating them. Therefore, if you have a possum that needs relocating, always check with the local government on their regulations and policies on how to do this properly. Guidelines and directions should be available on their website.

Additionally, many states have professional trappers who will catch and relocate the animals for you. Truthfully, this is not my preferred option, but it is available in many places. You should be able to obtain a list of licensed trappers and instructions on how to properly build boxes on the local wildlife pages or government websites.

Some general guidelines to consider when constructing the box, and again, check with your local government or wildlife centres if you need further information:

- The possum nesting box measures approximately 52 cm (height) x 25 cm (width) x 25 cm (depth). The post is 80 cm long. It is made of pine and weighs about 8.5 kg.

- The box should be placed in a shady position, with its opening facing away from the prevailing weather. Providing a summer and winter 'residence' is important because hollow-dependent mammals will change hollow locations depending on seasonal differences.

- If possible, place the box level with a branch in the tree to provide easy access.

- Securely fix the nest box to a tree in or close to your garden. Place it at least four metres (twelve feet) from the ground to keep it out of reach of domestic cats and dogs.

- Place the box in a position that is easy to access for monitoring and maintenance.

- It is recommended to attach the box using coated wire or thread the wire through a rubber hose where it contacts the tree. Creating a zigzag pattern in the wire at either end of the join will also allow for expansion as the tree grows.

Climate Change - Bushfires

One of the saddest things I have done is when I accompanied Greg, Michelle, and other members of various rescue groups across New South Wales on a "Black Walk" following a destructive bushfire ignited by someone not properly disposing of their cigarette butt. It took firefighters and first responders three weeks to properly contain the fire.

On the first day, it was safe for people to return to the area. Wildlife rescuers went into the area to look for wildlife that survived the fires, to euthanise animals that were in serious pain from burns or smoke inhalation, and to bury those who died in the flames. Since many of the adults thought that my accompanying them while they looked for injured wildlife would be too gruesome for me, they handed me a stack of metal bowls with several bottles of water and suggested I fill the bowls and put them in different locations for creatures that survived. It was the saddest day of my life.

It feels like no matter where we look, whether it's a news segment, school discussion, or even a simple conversation with our families, the topic of climate change is ever-present. While it can be overwhelming to witness such urgency, it's essential to understand what it means for our delicate ecosystems and the animals that inhabit them. Each story of change reflects the struggles and resilience of wildlife that deserve our empathy and action.

Climate change negatively impacts our world, leading to rising temperatures that cause multiple challenges. You may have noticed how the days seem to be getting hotter and that we haven't been experiencing the cold weather we used to. These changes can be concerning and are consequences of the ongoing climate crisis.

In Australia, many of us experience frequent and severe weather events, such as bushfires, floods, storms, heat waves, cold snaps, and droughts. It's heartbreaking to hear stories from our parents and teachers, who remember different weather patterns from their childhood. They might share their worries about the increasing number of bushfires or the prolonged periods of drought and intense flooding we're experiencing today. These personal experiences remind us that climate change is not a future issue we'll have to deal with 'later' it's happening now, affecting our communities and loved ones.

The potential long-term effects on wildlife are equally distressing. Animals and their habitats suffer from loss of homes, scarcity of food and water, and increased vulnerability to diseases. These changes lead to population declines and even local extinctions, which is a tragic loss for our planet.

One of the most alarming consequences of climate change is the rise in bushfires. I was seven years old during the devastating Black Summer Fires in 2019. Though my memories are a bit hazy, I've listened to the stories and concerns of the adults around me. They spoke of how those fires burned longer, ravaging vast areas of land and tragically leading to the loss of three billion precious animals. It's deeply upsetting to hear scientists warn that such catastrophic fires may become more frequent due to climate change. All of us feel the impact of these events, and it's a reminder of the urgent need to address this crisis together.

Unfortunately, there isn't much we can do to help the animals until the fires are extinguished and the fire department confirms it's safe to enter the affected area. However, we must remember that the effects of these devastating fires linger long after they have been contained, but there are still meaningful ways we can care for and support our wildlife after these difficult events.

In the aftermath of a fire, after authorities indicate it is safe to drive through these regions, do so cautiously and compassionately. For example, drive slowly because wildlife will be seeking food and shelter in these vulnerable zones. Pay attention to any animals that appear sick or injured, and look out for orphaned young if you come across a deceased parent.

Clearing away debris after a fire can significantly assist in the recovery process. Still, it's essential to do so carefully because many animals are lost after a natural disaster and look for shelter under fallen logs, rocks, and other debris. Inspecting these locations before moving or removing materials is important, as you might discover animals needing help. By being mindful of wildlife during cleanup efforts, we can ensure their safety and support the recovery of the local ecosystem.

One effective way to restore ecosystems where vegetation has been destroyed is to plant trees. Choosing native tree species well-adapted to the local environment helps to rebuild the habitat for animals and improve soil quality. Additionally, setting up bird nesting boxes in these regions provides safe havens for local bird populations, encouraging them to return and thrive. Ensure that boxes are placed in appropriate locations, away from predators and with access to food sources, to maximise their effectiveness in supporting bird life. By taking these actions, we help in the recovery of natural habitats and enhance biodiversity in our surroundings.

Surprisingly, it is important to avoid putting out food for wildlife, as doing so can unintentionally attract the animals you want to help *and* their predators. This practice can disrupt the natural foraging behaviours of local wildlife and lead to increased competition for food sources, which may unintentionally put these animals at risk. Additionally, attracting predators creates dangerous situations for smaller, more vulnerable species, jeopardising their safety. By not feeding wildlife, we help maintain the balance of ecosystems and for animals to recover in their natural habitats without the added threats posed by human intervention.

Please remember that even months after a bushfire, injured wildlife may still be suffering. You might encounter animals with burns on their paws or tails, other injuries that aren't immediately visible, or those struggling with infections, smoke inhalation, dehydration, or starvation. Each small action you take can make a significant difference in your recovery.

Australia's climate is known to be hot and dry, which shapes the lives of many of its native animals. For instance, kangaroos have a fascinating physiological trait: they do not sweat. This unique adaptation allows them to withstand high temperatures and go for extended periods without drinking water. Their bodies efficiently conserve moisture and have developed behaviours, such as being most active during the cooler parts of the day, to prevent further loss of water.

The name koala comes from an Indigenous Australian word that translates to "no water," reflecting the koala's remarkable ability to get enough liquid from its primary food source, eucalyptus leaves. These leaves provide just enough sustenance and contain the bare minimum of moisture necessary for survival.

However, the ongoing effects of climate change are increasingly challenging these well-adapted species. Rising temperatures and prolonged heat waves threaten their habitats and survival. The heat can lead to dehydration, even in animals already adapted to super-dry environments. Changes in weather patterns also impact the availability of food sources like eucalyptus leaves, thereby complicating the lives of koalas and other species that rely on specific plants for nourishment and, therefore, survival.

As temperatures continue rising and environmental conditions become more unpredictable, even the most resilient Australian animals face new and troubling challenges.

We know how our beloved animals can suffer from heat stress. If you notice your pet seeking shade or looking unusually lethargic and unresponsive, it could be a sign they are overheating. You might also see them breathing with their mouths open, salivating, or panting heavily. Here are some steps you can take to help wildlife in distress. First and foremost, do not approach the animals. Instead, monitor them from a distance.

1. **Provide Water**: If an animal shows signs of heat stress, place water nearby and consider using a sprinkler or misting system.

2. **Do Not Force Water**: If an animal approaches you seeking water, **DO NOT** pour the water directly into its mouth. This can fill the lungs of some animals and lead to pneumonia, which can be fatal. Instead, pour water into a shallow dish and allow the animal to drink at its own pace.

3. **Seek Help If Needed**: If the animal does not recover within a few hours, contact a wildlife rescue organisation for advice.

Certain animals, including possums, are particularly vulnerable to heat stress, and monitoring their behaviour closely during hot weather is essential. Usually, possums are nocturnal creatures that stay hidden during the day, often cosying up in hollows of trees or within roof cavities. However, when they experience heat-related distress, these animals may venture out into the open during daylight hours, which is unusual for them.

If you see a possum that seems lethargic, unresponsive, or unusually active during the day, it could be a sign of heat stress or that the animal is injured or orphaned. Keeping a safe distance and observing the possum's behaviour without interfering is crucial. Signs of a heat-stressed possum may include excessive panting, drooling, or difficulty moving.

In these situations, contact your local wildlife rescue hotline. They will provide professional guidance on assisting the possum safely or arrange for its rescue by animal rescuers. Your quick action will positively impact the animal's well-being during challenging conditions.

Koalas are generally not well-suited to high temperatures, and they can struggle in extreme heat. If you spot a koala at the base of a tree, tightly hugging the trunk, it's essential to recognise that this behaviour can indicate the animal is suffering from overheating. Such a position is not typical for koalas, who usually spend their time perched high in the branches. An overheated koala may require immediate medical attention to ensure its well-being and prevent serious health issues.

Observing these signs is important for the koala's survival, and quick action will help provide the necessary care.

Flying foxes face significant challenges regarding their inability to sweat. Unlike many mammals that use sweat as a natural cooling mechanism, flying foxes rely primarily on licking their fur and wings to bring on evaporative cooling. However, this method has limitations and can lead to dehydration and another dangerous condition called hypoglycemia if prolonged.

When ambient temperatures soar above 38 °C, conditions become especially hazardous for these creatures. At this temperature, the surrounding air becomes hotter than the flying fox's body temperature, making it impossible for them to effectively cool down and regulate their core body temperature. When faced with such extreme heat, flying foxes risk heat-stroke, significantly threatening their survival.

In response to rising temperatures, flying foxes show certain behaviours. They may begin to pant, a similar response seen in dogs while licking their wings to increase evaporative cooling. They instinctively move lower in the trees or descend to the ground to seek relief from the oppressive heat in the canopy.

As temperatures climb even higher, particularly around 42 °C, the biological processes within their bodies start to break down. At this critical point, flying foxes become increasingly susceptible to heat stroke, leading to severe consequences, including mass mortality, which is especially concerning for species already facing many environmental challenges. This combination of behavioural adaptation and the physiological limits of flying foxes under extreme heat underlines how vulnerable these animals are to climate change and rising temperatures.

The extreme drought and soaring temperatures are taking a toll on all of us, including our beloved native animals. While there may not be an immediate fix for these creatures' challenges, we can all try to understand the signs of their struggle and start making small changes to offer our support. Every little action we take will make a difference in their lives during these difficult times.

Habitat Loss

We often hear a lot about Habitat loss, and I learned firsthand what it meant and how it impacted our wildlife when I was at Michelle and Greg's one spring afternoon when Michelle received a phone call. A clothing store at the local shopping centre had a koala wandering around the aisles, and the clerk didn't know what to do. After Michelle hung up the phone, she grabbed her purse and keys and told me we were going for a ride. I looked at her quizzically.

"A koala is wandering around a store so we need to relocate him," she explained.

That was the funniest thing I ever heard, and I giggled. In a stern tone I had never heard Michelle use with me, she said, "There is nothing funny about this. That poor koala has no home and is wandering inside because it is lost." We quickly got to her truck and headed to the store.

We arrived at an adoring audience of several shoppers hovering around the unusual guest. "Thank you for contacting me," Michelle said, "because we are in the middle of the breeding season; males roam more frequently looking for a mate."

"How do you know this one is a male?" one of the observers asked.

"See the brown strip on the middle of its chest?" I excitedly jumped in, "That's a scent gland males have to mark their territory and attract mates," I said, proud to have been able to answer the question.

"That's right," Michelle nodded, and taking advantage of the audience, she continued, "mating season is during the warmer spring and summer months. Male koalas are on the move looking for a mate and grown joeys are leaving their mum looking for new homes, so you must be diligent when you are out and about during these months."

"What else should people be aware of during this time, Hannah?" Michelle asked me. Everyone's eyes turned my way. I knew the answer and turned towards them confidently.

53

"These months are when last season's joeys start exploring outside their mum's pouches for the first time, so people should be on the lookout for female koalas with joeys on their backs, and we all need to be extra cautious at this time," I added.

Michelle nodded and smiled with approval as she handed me the basket where she had carefully placed the koala. We carried it to her truck immediately and headed back to Michelle's.

"What now?" I asked.

"I am taking him home to examine and keep overnight for observation, and if everything looks okay tomorrow or the day after, I will take him to a gum plantation not far from here. I don't think he's hurt, but he is a long way from home."

"That is so sad," I said, holding Michelle's purse while she unloaded the pet carrier with the koala from her car. "I wish I could do something to help," I sighed helplessly.

Michelle looked at me and smiled, "Actually, there is something you can do. The trees koalas need for food and shelter are rapidly disappearing due to bush fires and land clearing. There's an urgent need to replace the lost habitat. Maybe you could organise a tree planting event where you and your friends from school could spend a couple of hours planting new trees for koalas."

My eyes lit up. "I love that idea," I exclaimed. "We can do it on a Saturday morning for a couple of hours, and maybe I can convince our science teacher to give us school credit for it," I continued excitedly.

"That is a great idea," Michelle told me.

I was so excited about this plan that on the way back to her place, I listed everyone I could invite to participate. Michelle had barely parked her truck when I ran into the house to tell Greg about my plans. "Greg, Greg, guess what I am going to do," I shouted excitedly, and before he had a chance to respond, "I am going to organise a tree planting day so koalas will have new places to live."

"That sounds like a great idea," Greg said smiling, "but you know a lot of work is involved. It is not just as easy as inviting people and showing up to plant the trees. First, you need to find an area where such a project is possible, and then you need to get permission from the property owners, maybe the government as well, then you have to get the supplies," he continued.

"Yeah, yeah, yeah," I said impatiently as he continued to reel off a list of everything that needed to be done.

"I'll make you a deal," Greg said, seeing my impatience about all the tasks involved, "I will find a proper place to host the event and work out all the details to obtain permission from everyone involved. You focus on getting people there, and once we know how many people to expect, you and Michelle can get the supplies we need. How does that sound?"

"I love it."

For the next three months, we organised my tree-planting event. We decided on a Saturday morning because it would be cooler and a non-school day. At first, it was not easy to convince my classmates and friends to get up at 8:00 on a Saturday morning to plant trees. Still, luckily, with my pleading of the importance and convincing my teacher to give extra credit to anyone who participated, I persuaded twenty-five people to come from my school.

While Greg worked out the "bureaucratic details" of finding a place for the event and getting permission, during the evenings and weekends after I finished my homework, Dad helped me make flyers to post in public areas within the city.

Because I am the only twelve-year-old on the planet whose parents won't allow her to be on social media, my parents, Michelle and Greg, and other members of the rescue group they belong to shared details about the event on their social media accounts, and encouraged their friends to do the same.

Three weeks before the event, Michelle called a local nursery to ensure they had enough seeds for us. Greg, Michelle, and I went to the nursery three days before the event to pick them up. The woman behind the counter shared her knowledge and advice. "Koalas are notoriously picky eaters, and even though there are over 600 different types of eucalypt in Australia, they will only eat two or three different types. The kinds of leaves koalas eat vary by region, so do not assume that if a koala in New South Wales eats one kind of leaf, a koala in Victoria will eat the same one.

"Therefore, always check with wildlife professionals, vets, or horticulturists about the appropriate leaves for the region before planting anything. It would be a shame to go through all the trouble of planting trees only for the koalas not to eat it."

Because koalas like a little variety, we purchased three different seeds for our big event.

Finally, the big day arrived. I was so excited I only got three hours of sleep the night before. We arrived at 7:00 to give us enough time to set up and get organised before people arrived. By 8:00, we had over one hundred people there! Not only did my friends and teachers come, but my friends brought their families with them, who also participated in the festivities. In only two hours, we managed to plant over a thousand trees.

We asked for a two-dollar donation to contribute to the cost of the seeds, but by the end of the day, we collected more money than we needed, so I gave the remaining money to Michelle and Greg to use for the animals at their sanctuary.

As we cleaned up after everyone else had left, I proudly announced my success. "Soon, koalas will have a home again," I said naively.

"I wish it were that simple," Michelle told me. "The work we did here today is a good start, but gum trees take time to grow, and even when they begin to grow, it will be seven or eight years before they are of significant use to koalas." Seeing the puzzled look on my face, she continued, "Koalas prefer fresh leaves, and those come from taller trees, so while the animals will begin to see some benefits in a couple of years, it will be several years before they reach the maximum benefit to be useful for koalas, but nevertheless, great work today. If we do nothing, nothing happens."

Scientists often claim habitat loss is the most significant cause of extinction. But what does "habitat" mean, and how does habitat loss occur? Habitat refers to a particular animal's natural environment and the resources it needs to survive, including food, water, shelter, and mating opportunities. When we talk about habitat loss, we are talking about the decline or elimination of these environments, making it hard for species to survive.

Habitat loss happens for many reasons, including logging, urban development, agricultural expansion, pollution, and climate change. These actions drastically change the landscape so that animals cannot survive in their natural habitats. For example, if a forest is cut down for timber or converted into farmland, the animals that depend on that forest for food and shelter are forced to leave.

The entire ecosystem is destroyed, so plant life, birds, and insects all disappear.

Occasionally, animals migrate to new locations for more favourable living conditions. Still, this process can be challenging because it may require crossing dangerous territories or competing with other species for limited resources. Unfortunately, not all animals are fortunate enough to relocate successfully. Many fail to find adequate food or shelter in their new surroundings and may ultimately die.

Since European colonists arrived in Australia, sixty-two native species have become extinct because of habitat loss and land clearing for different human uses. Today, the species most impacted by habitat destruction in Australia are the red goshawk, which has lost approximately 14,877 hectares; the grey-headed flying fox, which has experienced a loss of 13,522 hectares; the koala, subjected to a decrease of 13,053 hectares; the Australasian bittern, with 12,274 hectares lost;

and the regent honeyeater, which has seen a decline of 9,242 hectares of its habitat.

The issue of habitat loss is a deeply emotional and controversial topic in Australia. While many people genuinely want to protect our native wildlife, it's clear that much of their natural habitat is also desirable for human development. As human populations grow in these regions, there's often a sense that our needs should take priority over the homes of these animals.

Fortunately, there are compassionate ways to raise awareness about habitat loss without getting caught up in the debates. For example, the internet is filled with touching images and videos of koalas wandering anxiously through parking lots, trying to enter stores, or even climbing to the top of utility poles and fences. While many people might find these scenes "cute," it's essential to recognise the sadness behind them. These koalas are searching for safety and shelter because they have lost their homes due to habitat destruction.

By sharing this perspective, you can help others understand the real impact of habitat loss. Raising awareness in this way is a gentle and practical approach to educating people about the challenges our wildlife faces, and it encourages empathy for both the animals and the environment we share.

We can all play a pivotal role in minimising the impact of habitat loss on our native wildlife, and there are compassionate actions we can take together. One simple yet meaningful step is to ask your parents to plant a garden filled with local flowers, shrubs, and trees. This creates a welcoming environment for native birds, bees, and other animals, supporting the delicate balance of our ecosystems. Clearing away non-native weeds can also help our native plants thrive, allowing them to flourish and attract beautiful birds and butterflies, including some species that may be threatened.

If you know friends or family who enjoy camping, gently encourage them to prioritise safety by fully extinguishing campfires and properly disposing of cigarette butts, especially when spending time in bushland. Everyone must respect fire bans as they help protect our natural areas. Consider carrying a stove to minimise impact when bushwalking because many small animals depend on fallen wood for shelter and nesting.

For those with domestic animals like cats, dogs, or fish they can no longer care for, it's important to find them a new loving home. Please encourage your friends to consider rehoming with friends, selling, or taking them to the RSPCA rather than releasing them outdoors. This way, we prevent pets from ending up in pristine bushland far from their homes.

When fishing, please be mindful to return any tiny fish and allow them to grow. Also, be careful not to lose nets, lines, hooks, or sinkers in the water, as these significantly threaten countless marine life like whales, fish, birds, platypuses, and water rats.

If you encounter any threatened species, please encourage friends and family to share your observations or join a wildlife survey organised by dedicated research groups. The challenges faced by wildlife are often linked to human activities, but many organisations are actively working to engage the public in conservation efforts. For instance, when developers aim to clear an area for new housing, these organisations offer tools, such as apps, to help individuals report their wildlife sightings, noting which animals they see, how frequently, and at what times.

This collected data plays a crucial role in supporting their protection, as it allows organisations to highlight the presence of certain animals, like koalas or possums, in specific areas. They can use this information to support calls for better signage or reduced speed limits at intersections where wombats or kangaroos may cross. Together, we can all help to protect the extraordinary wildlife around us.

Vehicle Strikes

One Saturday morning, when I arrived at Michelle and Greg's house for my volunteer duties, I noticed that both looked tired and grumpier than usual. I thought I might have done something wrong, so I asked them if they were mad at me. "No, we're just tired. Last night was a full moon, and full moons are horrible for wildlife. Between 9:00 pm last night and 6:30 this morning, we received twelve calls about animals injured on the roads, and we spotted an additional four animals that hadn't been reported. Each time we returned home, we had to turn around for another call-out," Michelle said, yawning as she drank her coffee.

"I heard people talk about the importance of watching their driving habits between dusk and dawn but never about a full moon," I said.

"Yes, the increased light created from the full moon encourages sight-dependent animals to come out when they ordinarily wouldn't. Wildlife life rescuers do a pretty good job of educating people about the importance of driving carefully during dusk and dawn, but adding a full moon to their educational talks is something we could all better discuss."

One of the leading dangers to our wildlife is vehicle strikes. If you recall, it was after my dad brought Summer home after her mum had been killed by a car that inspired my passion for wildlife.

Cars are one of the most important modern conveniences for people. Few inventions have transformed our lives so dramatically as cars. Unfortunately, vehicle strikes are hazardous to our wildlife.

Vehicles are unfamiliar to wild animals; they lack the instinct or fear to remain safe around them. Each year, millions of native animals are injured or killed by vehicles while attempting to cross roads. Government reports estimate that ten million native birds, reptiles, and mammals die annually due to vehicle strikes.

Accidents can happen, even when we're careful. It's important to remember that police officers and rescuers understand this, too. If you hit a wild animal, report the incident immediately. Your quick response can make a difference for that animal, potentially saving its life.

Animals often don't show visible signs of injury, so having them checked by a professional is essential to their survival. Even if it seems like they're okay, like a koala that climbs up a tree after being struck, remember that climbing is instinctual for them. They may be hurt but still try to escape as a natural response.

If you see a kangaroo hop away after an accident, please take a moment to call the authorities. They will help locate the animal and assess any injuries. Your compassion and prompt action could be a lifeline for these creatures.

One of the most heart-wrenching challenges for wildlife caregivers is the hesitation people often feel after hitting a native animal. Whether it's fear of repercussions or simply not realising what has happened, many times, it's someone other than the driver who reaches out for help. When an animal is struck, it can suffer serious injuries that require immediate medical attention. Delaying a call for help can mean the difference between life and death for these vulnerable creatures. Even waiting five minutes can be too late for an animal in distress. Encourage your loved ones to reach out for help promptly and, if they can, stay with the animal until assistance arrives. Their compassion and quick action could make all the difference.

Unfortunately, accidents do happen as we share our planet with various species. It's a reality we all face. Being aware of this, we can modify our driving habits during these hours to be more careful, especially during full moons.

When driving in areas where wildlife is known to cross, we should slow down and remain vigilant, scanning the entire landscape rather than only focusing on the road ahead. Using high beam lights when it is safe will enhance visibility and help spot animals that may be nearby. In addition, if we encounter an animal on the road, braking firmly instead of swerving is crucial, as this helps prevent further harm to ourselves, other motorists, and wildlife.

Understanding wildlife patterns in our regions also creates a safer environment. For example, during the koala breeding season from September to February, these creatures may be more active in searching for mates. Being extra cautious during this time makes a significant difference in protecting them. We help create safer spaces for people and wildlife through awareness and compassion.

Let's Talk About Euthanasia

One evening, Greg and I went to check on a kangaroo that a member of the public said had been caught in a fence. The woman stayed and waited for us to arrive and was distressed. Greg told me when he parked the car, he could see the kangaroo had a broken tail from the accident and suspected the kangaroo would have to be euthanised.

He left me by the side of the road to talk to the distraught woman while he examined the injured kangaroo. As he returned to us, he shook his head, which I had learned meant the animal could not be saved. "I am sorry," he told the woman, "but with a broken tail, there is nothing we can do. Euthanising him is the most humane thing we can do."

The woman began to cry uncontrollably, threw a plastic bottle of water at him, and said some words I'm not allowed to say. She accused Greg of being a murderer and said, "I never should have called. I *knew* that's what would happen. Killing animals is all you so-called rescuers do." Unfortunately, I had seen similar situations when members of the public didn't understand practical rescue and release standards.

One of the most confronting and difficult conversations working with wildlife is around euthanasia. It used to make me sad when Greg or Michelle told me they had to euthanise an animal. They said that sometimes euthanasia was the most humane thing we could do because an animal suffering and in pain from serious injuries or illness could never survive in the wild. It is a difficult choice for many adult carers to accept, so this subject is tough for children.

I still sometimes try to talk them out of it if there is an animal I have grown especially fond of. Each time, they remind me not to be selfish and that wildlife rescuers always do what is in the best interest of the animal, not themselves.

As I have gotten older and more experienced with animal rescue, I have a better understanding than I used to. It is never an easy decision to make, but as my parents taught me, sometimes doing the right thing is the opposite of doing what is easy. It is sad but understandable that as part of my rescue work, I have talked to many adults as well as children who don't have the knowledge and experience we have and are unable to understand the difficult choices we make, nor why we have to make them. In their distress, they are often mean or judgmental to caregivers for euthanising an animal.

Please know it is heartbreaking for a caregiver to euthanise an animal they are committed to helping, and they only do so when they know the chances of an animal surviving are minimal and their suffering is unacceptable. They never make these decisions lightly, and when they choose euthanasia, it is based on years of expertise in this area, which can only come from experience and training.

Trust them; they dedicate their lives to helping and protecting the wildlife we love.

Thank You!

Sadly, our precious wildlife faces many threats, and it's impossible to discuss them all, so the examples in this book are a few of the most common. I'm grateful for being able to share how fortunate we are to live in a country with unique and extraordinary animals found nowhere else on Earth. Acknowledging that many of these fantastic creatures face serious threats today is sad but realistic.

While it may feel overwhelming to consider the challenges they face, it's important to remember that although we may not be able to solve every issue individually, every small step we take will add up to making a significant difference overall.

I encourage you to join me in this journey, knowing that our individual and group efforts will create a brighter future for these animals.

To help you remember what we've discussed, I've put together some resources with websites and phone numbers to share with your parents and teachers. These will offer more information and ways we can all make a positive impact. We must be their voice because they do not have one. Let's all be the positive change needed for the incredible creatures who share our world.

What If I Find an Injured Animal?

We have a big advantage living in a country filled with so much wildlife, but one of the disadvantages is that we often find injured creatures when walking to school, hiking in the bush, swimming in the ocean, or driving to work.

I learned from my experience with Summer that despite our best efforts, handling an injured or sick animal may do further harm to them and can sometimes be dangerous to us as well. Rescue organisations suggest people carry gloves, towels, pillowcases, cardboard boxes, hand sanitisers, and a torch in their car in case they need to help injured wildlife, and responders who come to assist.

If you find an injured animal, here are some things you can encourage and educate others to do:

1. **Keep Area Safe**: Remove pets, children, and cars from the area. This includes securing the scene without approaching the injured animal. For example, keep pets indoors and place cones near the road to alert drivers.

2. **Take Notes of Area**: Note the location and extent of the animal's injuries. Mention any landmarks, signs, or other identifiers to help rescuers or first responders locate you quickly. If you have a phone, downloading a free locator app can be a big help. The 'What3Words' app is an invaluable aid.

3. **Monitor from a Distance**: Watch the animal from a safe distance to protect yourself and prevent further injury. Only approach the animal if directed by a wildlife veterinarian or rescue group.

4. **Contact Professionals**: Call a local wildlife vet or rescue organisation to report the situation, seek guidance, and follow their advice.

5. **Handling Small Wildlife**: If you are helping a small animal like a possum or bird, a wildlife worker may tell you to use a pillowcase

or towel to wrap or cover it and place it in a secure box for transport to a veterinarian or wildlife caretaker.

6. You should not give the animal food or water until a wildlife rescuer tells you it's safe to do so.

6. **Wait for Help**: If possible, stay at the scene with the animal until help arrives.

These steps are easy but crucial for the survival of our wildlife, and they don't require a big time commitment or any knowledge about wildlife to do them. Following these guidelines keeps you safe while providing essential care for injured animals. Take action today, and be prepared. Your involvement matters and can literally save a life!

How Do I Identify An Injured Animal

Wild animals are typically afraid of humans, so we rarely have the chance to see them up close unless we visit a zoo or sanctuary. This can make it challenging to recognise when they are sick or injured. However, like humans and our pets, wild animals show signs they are in distress and need help. By learning to recognise these signs and sharing this knowledge with friends and family, you will help raise awareness. This way, if anyone encounters an animal showing signs it is in trouble, they can contact wildlife caregivers for assistance. These signs include:

- The animal may allow you to get close to it instead of running, hopping away, climbing a tree, or flying away.

- The animal may look tired or lazy.

- They might move slowly or show signs of pain, like panting or excess salivation.

- Animals that usually stay in trees, like flying foxes and koalas, may be found on the ground.

- Nocturnal animals that never come out during the day, like possums and wombats, may be seen during daylight hours.

Even if you don't fully understand what some things mean or how they appear, having this knowledge and sharing the information with adults or friends is a good first step. If they recognise these symptoms in an animal, they will be better equipped to seek help.

Resources - How Do I Get Help?

As you go through the links below, you'll see there are thousands of caring people who feel the same way as you, and will help you to become a wildlife warrior too.

The resources and contact information listed here are current as of the first printing of this book.

Australian Capital Territory

RSPCA ACT

ACT Wildlife at http://actwildlife.net

New South Wales

WIRES (Wildlife Information Rescue and Education Service)
http://wires.org.au

Australian Seabird & Turtle Rescue Inc http://seabirdrescue.org.au

Organisation for the Rescue and Research of Cetaceans (whales, dolphins, porpoises) ORRCA https://orrca.org.au

Friends of the Koala - Northern NSW Coast
http://friendsofthekoala.org

Northern Rivers Wildlife Carers INC. http://wildlifecarers.com

Byron Bay Wildlife Hospital https://byronbaywildlifehospital.org

Tweed Valley Wildlife https://Carers-tvwc.org.au

Dolphin Marine Rescue-Coffs Harbour
http://dolphinmarinrescue.org

Koala Conservation Australia, Inc. http://koalahospital.org.au

Koalas in Care--Greater Taree, Great Lakes & Gloucester
https://koalasincare.org.au

FAWNA NSW Mid North Coast LGAS of Midcoast, Port Macquarie, Hastings, and Kempsey http://fawna.org.au

WINC (Wildlife in Need) http://wildlifeinneedofcare.org.au

Port Stephens Koala Hospital http://pskh.com.au

Native Animal TRUST Fund Inc http://hunterwildlife.org.au

Wildlife Animal Rescue and Care Society (Wildlife Arc)
http://wildlife-arc.org.au

Bouddi Wildlife Inc. https://macmastersbeachprogress.com/bouddi-wildlife-fund

Ku-ring-gai Bat Conservation Society http://sydneybats.org.au

Sydney Metropolitan Wildlife Services https://sydneywildlife.org.au

Taronga Wildlife Hospital http://taronga.org.au

Manly Sea Life Sanctuary Sydney http://manlysealifesantuary.com.au

Northern Tablelands Wildlife Carers http://ntwc.org.au

Rescue and Rehabilitation of Australia Native Animals (RRANA) http://rrana.org.au

Wildlife Carers Network Central West Inc https://wildlifecarers.org.au 0408 966 228

Snowy Mountains Wildlife Rescue (LAOKO) http://laokosmwr.org

Native Animal Rescue Group (NARG) http://narg.asn.au

Saving our Native Animals (SONA) email: hello@sona.org.au

Wildcare Queanbeyan Wildcare Queanbeyan http://wildcare.com.au

Northern Territory - Alice Springs, Katherine

Wildcare Alice Springs https://facebook.com/WildcareIncAliceSprings 0419 221 128

Wildcare Clinic: https://wildcareinc.com.au

- Wildcare Inc:https://allpetsvet.com.au

- Ark Animal Hospital Yarrawonga: https://thearkvet.com

- Barkly Veterinary Practice, Tennant Creek 0447 471 399 barklyvet@gmail.com

- Darwin Mobile Vets: https://darwinmyvetservice.com.au

- Howard Springs Veterinary Clinic:
  https://howardspringsvets.com.au

- Litchfield Vets: https://litchfieldvet.com.au

- Parap Veterinary Hospital: https://parapvet.com.au

- Paul Arnold Bush Photos: https://paularnold.com.au (animal drop-off point only).

- University Avenue Veterinary Hospital:
  https://univets.com.au

Ark Aid: https://wildlifedarwin.org.au/work-with-rescue-groups

Katherine Wildlife Rescue Service, Rescue Hotline: 0412 955 336

Northern Territory Government, Darwin
Call Darwin Wildlife Sanctuary: http://dwsnt.com.au 0473 992 581

Queensland

RSPCA Queensland To contact the RSPCA:
1300 264 625 (1300 ANIMAL)

Wildcare Australia, For all wildlife emergencies in Gold Coast, Logan, Scenic Rim and Brisbane, please call our Volunteer Hotline on 07 5527 2444 https://wildcare.org.au/contact

- Wildcare (07) 5527 2444 - South East QLD - Brisbane, Gympie, Toowoomba & Gold Coast

- RSPCA QLD 1300 ANIMAL (1300 264 625) - All Areas

- BARN 0405 056 066 - Brisbane

- Pine Rivers Koala Care 0401 350 799 - Moreton Bay and North Brisbane areas

- QLD Wildlife Carers and Volunteers 0439 502 228 - Bundaberg

- Redland City (07) 3833 4031 - Koala Rescue and Wildlife Rescue Advice

- Mission Beach Wildcare Inc. 0439 687 272 - Far North QLD Cassowary Coast Cardwell to Innisfail

- Far North QLD Wildlife Rescue (07) 4053 4467

- WILVO's (07) 5441 6200

- Tablelands Wildlife Rescue Inc (07) 4091 7767 - Cairns and surrounding tablelands

- Wildlife Rockhampton 0429 469 453 - Rockhampton and Livingstone

Wildlife Rescue Queensland https://wrq.org.au/contact Moreton Bay Region 24-Hour Hotline 0478 901 801

Kerry's Wildlife Rescue & Care Inc. +61 431 674 016, Brisbane, Queensland Area

Wildlife Rescue Education and Rehabilitation: Murphy's Creek, Queensland +61 7 4630 5208

Wild Woman Wildlife Rescue, from Ingham to Cairns and as far north as the beautiful Atherton Tablelands.
https://wildwomanwildliferescue.com/contact
0474 205 500

Wildlife Rescue Service, Redlands Coast, Call (07) 3833 4031

https://redland.qld.gov.au/info/20253/native_wildlife_trees_and_pl
ants/620/wildlife_rescue_service

Koala Rescue, Queensland. Based on the Sunshine Coast, they provide services to wildlife hospitals and have no time frame or travel boundaries. Ray - 0423 618 740
Murray - 0431 300 729
Susan - 0466 439 947 https://koalarescueqld.org

South Australia

RSPCA SA: https://rspcasa.org.au

Fauna Rescue, Wildlife Hotline (24 Hours)
Phone: (08) 8289 0896 or Phone: 1300 KOALAS (1300 562 527)

Bat, including microbats and flying foxes, Rescue Hotline (24 hours)
08 8486 1139 http://faunarescue.org.au

Koala Rescue South Australia: +61 8 7226 0017, Glengowrie SA, Australia

Wildlife Welfare Organisation (SA) Inc., Goolwa & Fleurieu, +61 434 114 628, https://wwosa.org.au

Save Our Wildlife Foundation (SOWFI), +61 8 7120 6610, https://save-our-wildlife.org.au

Bat Rescue South Australia, Adelaide area, +61 475 132 093, https://batrescuesa.com

Kangaroo Rescue South Australia, https://kangaroorescue.com.au/about-us

Southern Koala and Echidna Rescue Ltd (SKER), Adelaide area, +61 435 056 252, https://sker.org.au

Adelaide Koala Rescue (AKR), +61 413 185 771, https://akr.org.au

Barossa Wildlife Rescue, Barossa Valley region. +61 402 646 574, https://barossawildliferescue.com.au/about-us

Adelaide and Hills Koala Rescue - 1300 KOALAZ Inc, +61 1300 562 529, https://1300koalaz.com

Kangaroo Sanctuary South Australia Inc, Wynn Vale, SA, +61 416 623 208

Koala Rescue South Australia, Glengowrie, SA, +61 8 7226 0017

Adelaide Koala Rescue (AKR), Adelaide Hills and Adelaide Metro Area, +61 413 185 771 https://akr.org.au

KOALA RESCUE, +61 474 737 283

Tasmania

Bonorong Wildlife Sanctuary, 0447 364 625 (0447 ANIMAL), https://bonorong.com.au/our-animals

Pademelon Park Wildlife Refuge, East Coast of Tasmania, 0400 378 055, https://pademelonpark.com.au/animal.facts

Andara Wildlife Sanctuary, Sharlene King: 0481120388, https://somethingmagical.com.au/index.php/andara

Penguin Rehab and Release, North West Tasmania, 0437 565 672, https://www.penguinrehab.org

Raptor Refuge, Kettering, 1800 727 867 (1800 RAPTOR), https://raptorrefuge.com.au

Raptor Care North West Phone, Wynyard, 0418 369 967,

North East Raptor Rescue, Lilydale +61 432 332 672

Victoria

Wildlife Victoria http://wildlifevictoria.org.au

Animalia Wildlife Shelter, Sand Belt Region, +61 435 822 699, https://animaliawildlife.org.au

The Wildlife Rescuers Inc, Melbourne Area, +61 417 506 941, https://wildliferescuers.org.au/about-us

Wildlife rescue and rehab statewide, +61 434 714 104

Wildwood Wildlife Shelter, Victoria Valley, +61 418 161 826

Murrindindi Ranges Wildlife Shelter Inc, Pheasant Creek, Victoria, · +61 430 440 286

ROWA Wildlife, Myrtleford area, +61 405 193 807, https://reachoutwildlifeaustralia.org/wildlife-rescue

Wallabia Wildlife Shelter, Goongerah, East Gippsland, +61 497 200 927

Dutch Thunder Wildlife Rescue, Koonoomoo, +61 417 560 910

Western Australia

Wildcare Helpline http://wildcarehelpline.org.au

Darling Range Wildlife Shelter, Orange Grove area· +61 8 9394 0885

Native Animal Rescue, Malaga, have a regional branch in Broome, +61 8 9249 3434, https://nativeanimalrescue.org.au

WA Wildlife Hospital, Bibra Lake, +61 8 9417 7105, https://wawildlife.org.au

PilRoc Retreat Wildlife Rescue Centre, Paynes Find, +61 418 919 773

Mandurah Wildlife Rehabilitation Centre, Dawesville, +61 89582 3938, https://mandurahwildlife.com.au

Kanyana Wildlife, Lesmerdie, +61 8 9291 3900, https://kanyanawildlife.org.au

Bridgetown Wildlife Rescue Inc, Balingup, +61 427 078 047, https://bwr.org.au

River Wren Wildlife Rescue, Stake Hill, +61 405 277 796

Wildlife Carers Australia-wide

Contact your local vet, use a search engine or the nearest library to find the local wildlife rescue centres closest to you. Share the information you find with your school library and class teacher to display in a prominent position.